My First
Book of
Nature

Trees

Victoria Munson

Published in paperback in Great Britain in 2019 by Wayland
Copyright © Hodder and Stoughton 2017

Wayland
Carmelite House
50 Victoria Embankment
London
EC4Y 0DZ

Editor: Victoria Brooker
Designer: Elaine Wilkinson

A cataloguing record for this title is available at the British Library.

ISBN: 978 1 5263 0156 7

Printed in China

MIX
Paper from responsible sources
FSC® C104740
FSC
www.fsc.org

Wayland, part of Hachette Children's Group and published by Hodder and Stoughton Limited.
www.hachette.co.uk

Acknowledgements:
iStock.com 7 Whiteway; 15 kn1; All other images and graphics, Shutterstock.com cover: tl Dani Vincek; tm SeDmi; bl Alekcey; tr D7INAMI7S; bm Anest; br Kulish Viktoriia; 02t Mark Heighes; 2b Linnas bottom; 3b Rigucci; 3t Gertjan Hooijer; 4 ileana_bt; 4 Noradoa; 5 Paveik; 6t stocker1970; 6b BenSkipper; 6 Brzostowska; 8b Maksym Bondarchuk; 8t RSOrton Photography; 9t Marius S. Jurgielewicz; 9b Nikolina Mrakovic; 10 kzww; 11t Andrew Roland; 11b Przemyslaw Wasilewski; 12 gubernat; 13t Bildagentur Zoonar GmbH; 13b chbaum; 14 Kletr; 15t Michal Zduniak; 16 Pixel Memoirs; 17b Hector Ruiz Villar; 17 Raymond Llewellyn; 18 Lucie Zapletalova; 19t billysfam; 19b Mike photos; 20 LFRabanedo; 21t Jukka Palm; 21b srekap;

Contents

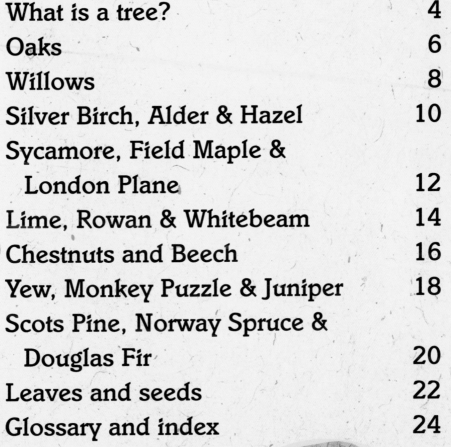

What is a Tree?

A tree is a plant with a large woody stem called a trunk. Trees have branches and leaves.

Roots grow underground and provide water and nutrients.

Trees are home to many different creatures. Birds and animals, such as squirrels, live among the branches. Insects can be found crawling under the bark.

This book looks at two groups of trees, deciduous and conifer.

Deciduous trees lose their leaves in autumn. The leaves are brightly coloured at this time. New green leaves grow in the spring.

Conifer trees do lose their leaves, but a little at a time so that the trees never look bare.

Many conifer trees are cone-shaped.

Oaks

There are a few different types of oak tree. The most common oak tree in the UK is the English oak. Its grey bark has deep ridges and cracks.

One oak tree can produce up to 50,000 acorns in a year.

An oak tree doesn't produce acorns until it is at least 40 years old.

Sessile oak trees have straighter branches and a more upright trunk than English oak trees.

Sessile oak acorns don't have a stalk.

Oak wood is very strong and has been used for thousands of years for shipbuilding and for house beams.

Turkey oaks look like other oak trees, but their leaves are thick and rough.

Turkey oak acorns have hairy cups.

Willows

Weeping willows are large trees found near ponds and rivers. Their long, narrow leaves hang, or weep, into the water.

Crack willow trees get their name because their twigs break off easily with a noisy 'crack' sound.

Crack willows have dark-green glossy leaves.

Goat willows are small trees mostly found near rivers and wet areas.

Goat willows have furry catkins that look like cat's paws.

In some countries, people use willow branches instead of palm branches on Palm Sunday.

Willow wood is used to make cricket bats.

Goat willows are also called pussy willows.

Silver Birch, Alder & Hazel

If you look at the trunk of a silver birch, you can sometimes see the bark peeling off in large strips.

Silver birch leaves are heart-shaped.

Silver birches get their name from their silver-coloured trunks.

Silver birches have long, dangling catkins called lamb's tails.

Alder trees grow best in damp areas such as wet woodland or near riverbanks.

Alders have round leaves and small, brown cones.

Hazel trees are small trees with round leaves.

Humans and animals eat nuts from hazel trees.

11

Sycamore, Field Maple & London Plane

Sycamore trees have smooth, pinkish-grey bark. Small green flowers appear in spring.

Sycamore flowers turn into winged seeds.

Sycamore seeds are often called helicopters.

Field maples are small trees. In spring, field maples have yellowish-green, cup-shaped flowers that hang in clusters.

Field maple sap is used to make maple syrup.

Often found in towns and cities, London plane trees make up more than half of the trees in London.

In winter, look for the London plane trees' seed balls.

Large pieces of grey bark flake off plane trees showing the creamy bark beneath.

Lime, Rowan & Whitebeam

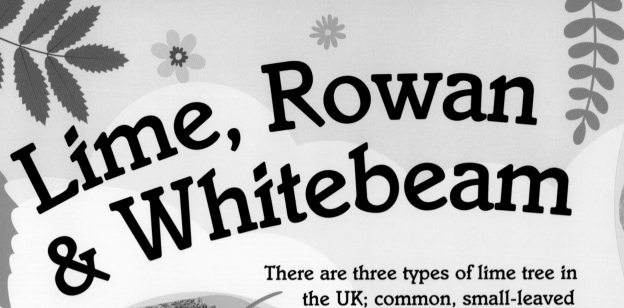

There are three types of lime tree in the UK; common, small-leaved and large-leaved.

All lime trees have heart-shaped leaves.

Lime trees attract greenflies and blackflies that feed on the leaves making them sticky.

Rowan trees are also called mountain ash trees because they grow high up on hills.

In spring, Rowans have sprays of creamy-white, scented flowers. By summer, the flowers have turned into bright red berries.

Whitebeam trees have oval leaves.

In spring, the undersides of a whitebeam's leaves look white because they are covered with white hairs.

In autumn, whitebeam trees are covered in red berries.

15

Chestnuts and Beech

To recognise horse chestnut trees in summer, look for trees covered in large upright spikes of white, or pale pink, flowers.

Horse chestnut trees are better known as **conker trees.**

Sweet chestnut trees have large oval-shaped leaves. In autumn, prickly cases protect tasty chestnuts.

Roasted chestnuts are sweet and delicious.

Beech trees have smooth grey bark.

Beech nuts are only produced once every four years.

A beech tree's trunk is large, but its roots don't grow very deep so they are often one of the first trees to fall in a storm.

Yew, Monkey Puzzle & Juniper

Yew trees are often found in graveyards. Some people cut yew trees into different shapes. Yew trees have flaky, red bark.

Yew leaves are long and narrow.

Yew leaves and berries are very poisonous to humans.

Monkey puzzle trees have sharp-pointed leaves.

They get their name because people thought its spiny branches would puzzle a **climbing monkey.**

In Chile, people eat the seeds from monkey puzzle trees.

Juniper trees have sharp, pointed leaves. They are found mainly in rocky areas.

Juniper berries used to be burnt at Halloween to scare away evil spirits.

Pine, Spruce & Douglas Fir

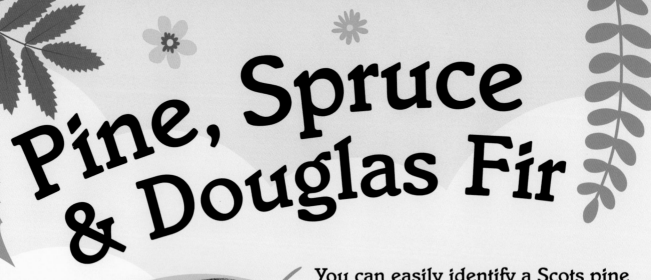

You can easily identify a Scots pine tree because the lower part of the trunk is grey while the upper part is rust-red. No other pine tree is like this.

Squirrels and birds eat the seeds in pine cones.

Wood from Scots pine trees is used for telegraph poles.

Norway spruces have needle-like pointed leaves. Their cones have diamond-shaped scales.

Norway spruces are tall, straight trees, better known as Christmas trees.

Some Norway spruce trees can live for up to **1,000 years.**

Douglas fir trees are one of the tallest trees found in the UK.

Douglas firs have long cones that dangle down from branches.

Leaves and Seeds

Look at the shape of leaves to help you to identify trees. Here are leaves and their seeds from some common trees.

1 beech

2 sycamore

Glossary and Index

catkin a spike of tiny flowers that hang down from tree branches

cone the fruit of evergreen trees

nutrient something that helps plants and animals to grow

sap the liquid inside trees that carries nutrients and water

3 lime

4 oak

5 horse chestnut

23